I0488071

A Production of TimothyTuohy.com

Artificial Intelligence

Healthcare Information Technology

Total Value Delivery

Timothy Tuohy

Copyright

Copyright 2019

© As "Artificial Intelligence Healthcare Information Technology Total Value Delivery"

All rights reserved by Timothy Tuohy.

No part of this book may be reproduced or retransmitted in any form or by any means, graphic, electronic, or mechanical, including photocopies, scans, recording tape, or by any data storage and retrieval system, without the express written permission of Timothy Tuohy.

Second Edition

For additional information:

Go to: http://www.timothytuohy.com

ISBN 978-0-359-97720-8

Cover art courtesy Jackson Health System

Dedication

This book is dedicated to my grandson. He was diagnosed with leukemia at the age of ten months. It was this seminal event that caused me to fully understand the importance of the work we are doing in Healthcare and in Healthcare Information Technology.

The orange bar on the cover of the book and the orange color of the dialog boxes herein are all as the result of my desire to call attention to Childhood Cancer and specifically to leukemia in children.

Artificial Intelligence –
Health Care Information Technology Total Value Delivery

Table of Contents

Artificial Intelligence –
Health Care Information Technology Total Value Delivery

Preface

This is the beginning of a very long journey. This is the beginning of another battle front in the battle for a cure. This project will determine, in my opinion, if we as humans, in concert with our technology, can find answers to disease that up until now we have never been able to find.

Can we learn from the revolution that's been taking place in computer science for the last two decades? More and more we see computer programs that learn. Software can adapt to behavioral leads automatically. We have programs that can recognize people's faces, drive cars, recommend movies to watch based on things that we've already searched for in our Amazon account. All these things make it much easier for us to live. It's as if we have our own personal assistant watching out for us and making recommendations based on what our behaviors have been in the past. However, until that time when we can use these types of technologies to anticipate the causes of diseases and the cures for diseases, we really have done nothing more than use the technology to make ourselves more luxuriated.

In days gone by it was up to an individual programmer to define what a computer had to do. Coding an algorithm in the programming language was the task of an individual, of a person, the data contained the fabric that was stitched together by the programmer to get an outcome. They have remained much the same since the middle of the last century when they were first invented. However, computers are no longer just massive calculators relegated to do finances and accounting and other numeric structures that make our lives easier or other actions repetitive in their nature. Only when we move past using computers simply for accounting, will we be providing health care professionals the total value of

3

what we are capable of as a race, as a species and with our technology.

This book is not intended to provide the answers to the questions, on the contrary this book is designed to raise more questions.

This book is designed to give an overview of what I think will be the most challenging project of my entire career. And maybe the most challenging project that information technology as a profession has undertaken since the years of the Second World War, when Alan Turing invented the mechanical computer to help break the code used by the Germans and thereby introduced computerized information for the first time to alter the course of history.

Let's be very careful to communicate how important I believe it is that what we've done with information technology up until now has been a huge assistance to humanity as we have run our businesses. In health care the idea of assuring that we have the right medicine for the right patient at the right time with the right treatments for the right fee is tantamount to the survival of the health care industry. Many countries have socialized medicine because they could not get control of the spending related to health care and as a result, their respective health systems have suffered. This is not a statement on the pros or cons of health care being socialized. In his book "Hacking Health Care" Fred Trotter shows the importance of assuring that the billing is handled properly. (Trotter, 2013) It is not my intention to discount the value that we bring to the health care industry by assuring that the billing is correct.

However, until such time as we are also using the data that is being collected to provide insights into the causes and cures of diseases, we are not providing the total value that we should be bringing to the table in health care information technology.

This book is not a treatise on the advantages or disadvantages of any single type of technology. It is not intended to be a cookbook on how to assemble and use the artificial intelligence technologies and constructs to provide answers to the questions that we haven't yet learned to ask. This book is simply a proposal that we use this technology that we have, to search the data that we have, to define the answers to the questions that we have not yet learned to ask. The question I will focus on during this process is, "what is the cause of and are there better cures than chemotherapy and the damaging outcomes the chemotherapy inflicts on the patients particularly as it applies to infant leukemia?"

For the last two years prior to writing this book, I have been the IT Project Manager associated with a two-billion-dollar construction project at Jackson Health System in Miami Florida. We are building a new one hundred bed community hospital, a new state of art eighty bed Rehabilitation hospital, while we are renovating all our existing hospital facilities to bring them to the most current standards. My focus throughout this project has been to establish sufficient IT infrastructure to leverage the data that we collect for the project outlined in this book.

I want to thank you for picking up a copy of this book and reading it. I want to thank Jackson Health System and particular leaders within Jackson Health System who have helped me to understand many of the things that tie this all together both as a business and as a place of healing. I want to thank Carlos Migoya, Mark Knight, Mike Garcia, Bill Seed, and Scott Judd for believing in me and giving me the opportunity to continue this great work. I want to specially call out thank you to David Rockowitz, Ginger Adler, Danny

Anderson, George Rosello, Luis Encinosa, and Angel Calzadilla. There are so many dedicated, educated, committed, and loving people in this health system who have assisted me in the successful completion of so very many projects, like Mike Dye, Jerachmeel Bassette, Valerie Durden, Randy Fleury, Priscilla Lopez, Sandra Rico, and Janice Gonzalez, that I cannot individually name them all. I want to apologize to everyone I have not mentioned here who deserve mention. All of these have been 'there' for years pursuing excellence in health care without expectation of special recognition or even thanks.

Most importantly I'd like to thank my daughter, Kira, her husband, Carl, my grandson, Ellis, and my special little granddaughter, Clara, who has suffered so much as a byproduct of infant leukemia that attacked her baby brother. I want to pass special blessings to my daughter and son-in-law for persevering through the last two years of difficulties in total faith and in total love. I'd like to thank God for sending along my other grandson, Coen, who will never really know the impact of this dread disease. He is so full of joy and he is a true example of what Jesus meant when he said, "unless you become like a little child."

I want to thank all the doctors and nurses on the team. For the technicians who performed countless studies and for the environmental services people who kept the hospitals and clinics clean and free of infection.

Artificial Intelligence

Health Care Information Technology
Total Value Delivery

Chapter 1 – The Reason

He stopped on the landing of the seventh floor to catch his breath. It had been a week since hurricane Irma had made its slow pass over Miami. Though the electricity had not been returned to his apartment, he had received an email notice that the water was back on. A shower, even though cold would be welcome. He had been at the hospital for a week, sleeping in his office, spraying himself with deodorant and cologne – he referred to it as a "GI shower". Yes, a shower would be a welcome change. It was Sunday. He saw the crew downstairs working to restore the electricity in his building today. Maybe he could sleep at home in the air conditioning tonight ... in his own bed.

When he opened his apartment door there was a smell of rotting meat. He had simply forgotten to empty his refrigerator. Still, it was an alarming odor.

Monday came as Mondays do. He returned to work and as he was walking across the Jackson Memorial campus his cellphone rang.

"I.T." He answered with his work greeting.

"Dad?" He could tell by the quavering in her voice that his daughter was scared. "The baby is really sick. We're taking him to the hospital. They're going to run some tests."

Tuesday came; again, he was walking across the campus, still worried by yesterday's call, he called his daughter, he could tell she was frightened, she was a nurse, if she was scared, it was serious.

"We haven't heard yet," she told him. "When we do, we'll call."

Wednesday came, again he was walking across the campus when the phone rang.

"I.T., this is ..."

This time it was his son in law. "Come" was all he said.

He was on a plane early the next morning. When he arrived at his daughter's house he was greeted by his son in law's aunt and his two-year-old granddaughter. How does one explain this to a two-year-old?

The level of damage that occurred as a result of this illness that not only struck this baby, but this entire family is immeasurable. The devastation was immeasurable. The psychological impact on a two-year-old when her baby brother is struck by leukemia ... when mommy and daddy are suddenly called away to the hospital ... with no explanation ... for an unknown duration is tantamount to a death in the family and just as overwhelming. A two-year-old does not have the mental tools to deal with it. Her little developing brain has no method, apparatus, or experience on which to call. The adults don't either, how does one deflect the blow to this little girl? (Marusak, 2019)

As the story begins to unfold, we find the family in the hospital for five weeks. That ten-month-old baby was subjected to an entire five weeks regiment of chemotherapy immediately upon the discovery that he had leukemia. Of course, being an information technology guy, he began to do some research. What he found was alarming. What he found was we were treating this ten-month-old baby on a protocol based on a 1970s study. He found that new technologies had not been developed to fight cancer since the 1940s.

He knew we were looking for answers but there were no answers today. There were no answers outside of the world it existed since the 1940s.

During the period called the "induction", he was sitting cross legged on the floor in the hospital room in the UCHealth Anschutz Children's Hospital in Aurora Colorado, it's September and it's already a little chilly. He is here because his ten-month-old grandson has contracted infant leukemia. He is sitting cross legged on the floor because his grandson is on the floor. His grandson has a large bruise on his forehead that is a telltale sign of the problems that blood cancer causes in infants. The baby is just learning to crawl. He's just a tiny little guy and he crawls over, climbs up on his legs and sits on his lap. It's a very special time in a very special moment.

No family should ever have to be faced with the idea that their ten-month-old son or grandson has leukemia. He looks at this little child who's done nothing wrong ... who's done nothing to deserve this ... who has been in the world only ten short months ... he look across the room at his daughter ... she's done nothing to deserve this ... she been an exemplary mother ... she's a nurse she knows how to handle medical situations. One does not often contemplate the generational impact of cancer, but this was his daughter whom he could not help, with his grandchild whom he could not help. This situation has hit his family like a nuclear weapon.

He knows they are not alone. There are families in this hospital at this same time whose children had also been similarly diagnosed. He knows that there are other families across the globe that are faced with similar problems.

Sadly, statistics are not issued in terms of survival rates. They issue statistics in 'event free' survival rates. The problem is the events are far reaching, everything from brain development to bone issues. (NIH, 2018)

We can do better than this.

It is not all an issue of infant leukemia, it could also be some other dread disease for which they have no cure, but because infant leukemia is what affected me that is what I'm going to use as the example in this book. The story above is mine, and that of my family.

Each generation fights with the tools shaped by the preceding generations – General James Mattis

---

Proposal Based

This book is a proposal ... a research proposal ... a proposal to change how we look at and how we think about what we are doing in health care information technology.

For years we have been collecting data in the form of paper medical records, film X Rays, digital X Rays, cards that we send home with people, and more recently electronic medical records that we have kept on every item of every patient that we have seen. The problem is that until recently no one has really tried to keep these records together or make them portable to the population. HIPAA has done a great deal for that however the doctor's medical records that we have at my doctor here in Colorado Springs does not necessarily make it to my doctor in Miami Florida. Indeed, while the doctor here in Colorado Springs keeps splendid electronic medical records, they are propriety to that medical facility. The first and most important part of this quest for answers is based on access to that data. To as much data as we can possibly have access to.

I am sitting here on the balcony of my apartment looking over the Front Range of the Rockies and Pikes Peak with a headset on dictating to Microsoft Word - writing this book. As I dictate Word is auto saving this to the cloud in the form of "One Drive" that I also have.   I have the ability in "settings" to share these cloud files with anyone else who has Office 365 - I don't know if I could share it with someone who has a Google drive or any other shared device without making it a little bit more difficult but that's not the point ... the point is ... it can be done and this ability to share data through the internet is crucial to the success of this project. This level of technology is available now.

This is a proposal to use artificial intelligence to find the answers to questions that we may not even know to ask. The question that burns in my mind is what is the cause of infant leukemia? I believe that through the years we have collected the data that would give us the answer period.

The data stretches back for many years. Doctors who were well trained, deeply committed, and thoroughly caring about their patients have been writing down their observations, diagnoses, treatments, and outcomes through all this time. These are not people who were merely showing up because it was their job. In countless hospitals and medical schools across this nation and across the globe the best doctors in their respective regions have been logging their observations, symptoms, treatments, successes and failures, first on paper then electronically. This data is available to us. These doctors are people who care about healing, they care about the health of their patients and community.

I believe that in this vast matrix of data we have the answers already for the question "what causes infant leukemia?"

These are some discussion points on the value of the data we are collecting.

- We have been collecting data for years.

- Doctors are now and have been for years creating medical records that are as accurate and descriptive as they know how to make. These include their research into the diseases and diagnoses.

- Much of this data is in written format on paper.

- For the last few years this has been electronic.

- I believe the answer to the questions are already in our possession in these records.

- These records are too large for an individual or group of individuals to search and find the answers. I don't believe humans can do this efficiently and make the links between the connections. (Remember the Indian proverb of the blind men and the elephant?)

- I believe with Natural Language Processing we can begin to translate these written medical records in usable machine discernible data sets that can feed the Machine Learning engines to sort for meaningful information.

- I believe with these information data sets and artificial intelligence we can develop the questions and get the answers to "what causes infant leukemia?"

- I believe with these information data sets and artificial intelligence we can develop the questions and get answers to "what is the method and medicine that best presents a cure for infant leukemia?"

- I believe with these information data sets and artificial intelligence we can develop the questions and get the answers to "how do we know the baby is cured of infant leukemia?"

- I believe with these information data sets and artificial intelligence we can develop the questions and get the answers to "how do we eradicate infant leukemia?"

- While I have been focused on the project to cure infant leukemia, I believe with these information data sets and artificial intelligence we can develop the questions and get the answers to "how do we cure any of the dread diseases in the human experience?"

Only when we are using the data we are collecting to provide solutions to healing (not just financial accuracy) will we be providing Total Value Delivery.

It can be argued that behind this 'big data' and its amazing intricacy there lies unpretentious explanations. Although the data is big, it can be explained in terms of relatively simple models, a finite set of hidden features and their interactions. (Alpaydin, 2016) Defining and delivering that sample data set, that representation of the total population of data will be one of the outcomes of this project.

In a final note for this chapter, I want to give credit to a couple of other books that have heavily influenced this proposal, this book, this call to action. The first is General Stanley McChrystal's work titled "Team of Teams" and General James Mattis' work titled "Call Sign Chaos". It is important, I think that one should realize, in addition to seeing this as a project, I see this as a battle. This is a battle against cancer. The lessons, algorithms, and outcomes we uncover through this great work will benefit countless other such battles against treatable and untreatable diseases humanity encounters. Both these exemplary military leaders share how they developed their leadership in the unusual, dynamic, stochastic manner that we will need to exploit in this project if we are to be successful in defeating this enemy that wants to live in our human bodies.

This work will not succeed with a team of shallow workers, that is those that will succeed in this team will not be easily distracted by the technologically enhanced task driven work that the Information Technology industry has declined into. In his book "Deep Work", Cal Newport describes the importance of developing our ability to concentrate – to THINK. (Newport, 2016) This book was on General David Goldfein, U.S. Air Force Chief of Staff, reading list for March 2019, so I picked it up. If we are to succeed in the battle against Infant Leukemia, we will need to think jointly as do the Army, the Marines, and the Air Force. By this I mean, we will need to attract 'deep thinkers' who understand the value of working deeply and approaching things in teams.

Chapter 2 - Artificial Intelligence

For many of us, when we think of the term "artificial intelligence", our minds automatically go to science fiction because we're a television-based generation. However, those of us who have been in the information technology field for a long period of time know that artificial intelligence dates to the 50s maybe even the 40s. When I propose that we build an artificial intelligence to define the answers to the questions of where do these dread diseases come from, how can we stop them, how can we cure them, it sounds like it might be some futuristic "pie in the sky" dream when it is rooted in the very foundations of computer science's earliest days.

For the purposes of this book I am using the definition of artificial intelligence as I came to understand it from Doctor Tom Malone, Professor at MIT Sloan: "The term 'Artificial Intelligence' is notoriously hard to define." Doctor Malone stated in an interview in the course Artificial Intelligence: Implications for Business Strategy. "Sometimes, for example, people use it to mean things that are hard for computers to do, like understanding English, as opposed to things that we already know how to do with computers, like accounting." He went on to explain that Artificial Intelligence was merely machines behaving in a manner that appears intelligent.

Computation isn't changing things, its changing everything. The big changes are recent, suddenly machines are capable of the speeds of computation and applied technologies that will help us reach what many computer scientists refer to as the 'Turing Test' designed by Alan Turing in 1950. (Turing, 1950) We haven't changed the human ability to think of algorithms we have learned how to build machines that can compute them.

Upon asking the question that is credited for starting the research into artificial intelligence in his paper "Computing Machinery and Intelligence", Alan Turing put forward a test in which an interrogator would be unable to determine if the

---

*Actual human computers really remember
what they have got to do.
– Alan Turing*

---

responder was a human or a machine. One of his many observations pointed out that human computers remember what they have to do. (Turing, 1950)

Perhaps artificial intelligence started in Dartmouth College with a small team of researchers. Their names were McCarthy (Dartmouth College), Minsky (Harvard University), Rochester (IBM Corporation), and Shannon (Bell Telephone Laboratories). On August 31, 1955 they submitted a proposal that every aspect of learning could be thoroughly and accurately described so that computer programs could be developed to help humans solve problems. (McCarthy M. R., 1955)

Marvin Minsky published a paper in 1960 while he was at Massachusetts Institute of Technology under contract to the United States Air Force titled 'Steps Toward Artificial Intelligence", I lean heavily on this paper in this book. (Minsky, 1960) We will use the problems he introduces as the criteria of our project.

We need data

Let's think about it for a moment. For the last 100 years Jackson Memorial Hospital has been a hospital in Miami, it's not the oldest hospital in the country by any stretch of the imagination, but it is my point of reference since that's where I've been for the last several years. For the last century the doctors have worked tirelessly to cure disease. One of the early wards of Miami City Hospital, as it was once called, was a Tuberculosis Ward, the objective being to cure tuberculosis. I must believe that Doctor Jackson, for whom our health system is named, was diligent, detailed, and well documented in his work. I must believe he and his team were consummate, caring professionals. I believe they were doing everything they could to win the battle. I believe they left behind volumes of handwritten records otherwise known as data.

Jackson Memorial Hospital has long been associated with the University of Miami Miller School of Medicine. For all these many years of association together, is it any wonder that doctors and researchers at the University of Miami working in Jackson Memorial Hospital have collected data on all sorts of diseases? Of course, much of this data was recorded in the format of written medical records, logs and journals. Truly, rooms full of data on paper exist. Not only do these written records exist here, they exist in every major medical center in the world.

OR
do we just forget about all these written records
and use only the electronic records more recently
collected?

How do we gain access to this data? It is too much for humans to read through, and even if we had the resources to pay people to read through it, the boredom of doing so would lead to errors in assimilating the data into something useful. It would be like reading the entire unabridged Webster's Dictionary of the English Language. Further, what good would it do to simply read through it? For it to be meaningful, it must be digitized.

Similar to the early years of information technology when Turing, Minsky, McCarthy, Newell, and Simon (McCarthy J. , 2006) were projecting artificial intelligence methodologies but didn't have the hardware technology to pursue the ideologies that they had developed; I believe that doctors early on made observations and hypothesis about diseases that they had neither the ability nor the technology to cure. I believe the observations made in that old handwritten data that they inscribed or typed into their records has value to us now. I think that discounting those early days of medical records would be as impactful as discounting the work of the 1955 Dartmouth Summer Research Project. (Kline, 2011) We are doing ourselves a disservice and are selling ourselves short on valuable meaningful data.

But what do we do with it? How do we get our hands on this data and make it something that we can use in the artificial intelligence constructs we are going to build, where we could derive some meaning from the sheer massive volume of data that has been collected over the last century?

First, we would have to have access to the files. Many of the old files have been transferred to microfiche, scanned into portable document format, or copied into files as pictures. Some of the files are incomplete or severely damaged. Still, we would need access to as much of this data as we could realistically get access to.

Unlike electronic medical records – paper medical records are very difficult to de-identify. How do we make something that is recorded specifically for an individual and saved by that individual's name be de-identified?

We'll come back to the data later.

Artificial Intelligence Constructs

Artificial Intelligence has many sub-parts of technology. I think for this project there are five major components, I am borrowing them directly from Marvin Minsky's paper "Steps Toward Artificial Intelligence" (Minsky, 1960)

1. Search.
2. Pattern Recognition.
   a. Natural Language Processing – NLP
   b. Computer Vision
   c. Human life – my addition
3. Learning
4. Planning
5. Induction

Marvin did not have some of the information we have today on machine learning, which is included in each of these steps toward delivery of this project successfully. Therefore, in this book, a "construct" is the algorithms and hardware, as well as methods, procedures, and application.

Not about me

In writing this book I have spent many hours reviewing countless publications, books, academic papers, and journals. Many of these are hypothetical, theoretical, and idealistic. This book should be none of these. This book is not designed to show how much I know about the subject of artificial intelligence. All that would do is convince the novice and the proficient professional that I was a novice. I propose to lead a team in an agile project methodology I outlined in my 2017 book. (Tuohy, 2017) This will by necessity be broad based, wide ranging, heavily collaborative project. This project will be focused on finding the cause and cures for infant leukemia. I believe this process will unlock the method of applying this same technology to learn the cause and cures of any number of currently uncurable, or other dread diseases. I encourage anyone who would understand to read the reference materials listed in the Bibliography, you may come to a different conclusion than I, but it will be an informed conclusion.

Chapter 3 – The Data

The key is data. There is currently a data quake occurring from many sources creating a tsunami of information. Similarly, the volume of the data is too great for humans individually or in teams to be able to assimilate it into meaningful knowledge.

Types of data

- Laboratory study reports
- Paper records
- Individual records
- Peer reviewed research papers
- Medical Journals
- Records from doctor's offices
- Biomedical Devices
- Clinical Trials
- Electronic medical records
- Files from medical equipment
- Files from imaging equipment
- Wearable device data
- Video
- BLOG and VLOG
- Medical equipment recorded data
- DICOM data
- Exoskeleton data
- Sensor data
- Email

Sources of data

- Academic Papers and Journals
- National Institutes of Health
- Universities
- Health Systems

- Hospitals
- EMR Manufacturers
- Individual donors
- Social Media
- Internet search

Methods of assimilating data

- Individual permissions (sign in question "would you be willing to assist ..."
- Deidentified data collected from EMRs
- Scanned written documents assimilated through NLP
- WiFi from tablet and handheld devices
- Bluetooth from personal wearable devices
- Internet of Things devices

Normalization of data

- Field definition, size, data type
- Upper – lower case
- Numeric – non-numeric
- Special characters
- Unknown characters
- JPG vs PDF

If all the handwritten medical record available were stored in a single room, can you imagine how large a room it would be. The handwritten records of the ages, the early dictated and typed records stored in various locations fill basement archives worldwide. Years ago, I owned a medical transcription business, we worked around the clock transcribing the handwritten records of the various doctor's offices that were our customers into digital format records, stored in Word Perfect format. Word Perfect was one of the better word processing programs (of the time). This program, still available on Amazon, was also the choice of attorneys. I do not know what became of those records, but I wonder how hard it would be to assimilate that data into something we could use in our project. I am sure most of it was printed, stored in a paper file and the media it was recorded on was overwritten by the next batch of work.

Some of the early typed material would be easier to digitally assimilate than the handwritten records, scanned in and marked though OCR type programs to digitize that data into something that is usable but even this is a daunting task and OCR was never that wonderful at digitizing typed letters. So, what do we do?

In many environments, companies are hired to scan the thousands of paper documents into PDF libraries. These too can be digitized with programs to recognize and record characters. There are also treasure troves of data stored on microfiche, how can we access this data?

This is where NLP comes into focus. NLP is Natural Language Processing it has number of forms that are being presented in the artificial intelligence world, we will discuss them later in the book.

Every health system is heavily dependent upon technology as well as highly educated, specially trained, and superbly intuitive people. As I write this book, I am working with Jackson Health System in Miami Florida. Jackson is directly affiliated with the University of Miami (UM), Florida International University (FIU), Barry University, and Miami-Dade College (MDC). Jackson is the largest county hospital in the United States, tied for second place as the largest hospital in the United States and the eighth largest hospital in the world. Among the Jackson Health System business units is the Miami Transplant Institute which is the second largest transplant facility (by procedure) in the United States. It is home to Ryder Trauma Center, consistently the top-rated level one trauma facility in Florida. So complete is the trauma program, the US Army trauma physicians are trained at this facility.

There are many talented researchers in universities all over the world who are coming up with so many insights that have value. How many of these are interconnected and the linkages are invisible to us because we do not see the patterns yet? In his article titled "A casual mechanism for childhood acute lymphoblastic leukemia, Doctor Mel Greaves identified what he thought was a possible cause of the disease. (Greaves, Aug 2018) However, he also pointed out that Leo Kinlen may have come to the same conclusion based on a different field of study. Doctor Greaves is an evolutionary scientist while Doctor Kinlen is an epidemiologist. (Kinlen, Dec 1988)

In his article Doctor Greaves recognized the Doctor Kinlen had seen the same problem but had associated a different root cause in his analysis. This is exactly the type of situation that exists in the research that is being performed and I believe is something that we can use artificial intelligence to assist us in connecting. These two reports published thirty years apart were discovered in a single laboratory research operation headed by Doctor Greaves and his talented researchers. How many more of these cross references exist through the decades of research that have been completed by multiple groups of talented researchers?

The idea that there are individuals that are performing this level of research is mind boggling. How much more could we be doing if we, as a group of interlinked groups, a team of teams, (McChrystal, 2015) if you will, were interlinked using artificial intelligence and the Internet. The data is so immense the machine learning will be required just to reach the state of normalization. This project will employ artificial intelligence pattern recognition across multiple methods of research, disciplines, professions, nations, continents, languages and even religious beliefs that are too broad for humans too rapidly link what has been learned and published.

There is an additional observation to made here. These two independent researchers came to approximately the same conclusion from two separate viewpoints. Humans are notoriously biased. We tend to look at things through the lens of our experiences, history, emotions, education, training, faith and belief systems. Among the things that we must do in this project is develop methodologies to train

---

Nothing happens by magic even though it may appear to be magic when you don't know what's happening in the background.

---

the algorithms in our machine learning processes within artificial intelligence to cross reference the various biases to look at the root cause from as many angles as possible.

Translational Medicine (TM) has at its core three pillars, they are the Bench (referring to the laboratory), the Bedside, and the Community. (David Abramson, 2019) Recent changes in research-application workflows are dramatic. This has been driven by greater availability and increasing scales of data obtained through experimentations as well as observation of outcomes. Driven by the ability to model phenomena more holistically, and the availability of real time data processing, biomedical manufacturers, health care providers, clinicians, and care givers are all looking to translate the data these new technologies provide into more effective and efficient healing experience. Similarly, there is a movement in Computer Science to model a similar approach to accelerate the impact of computer science research overall. (Steven D. Pyle, 2019)

An example of the tectonic changes that are occurring within the health care industry can be seen a Jackson Health System in Miami Florida. Until 2011 Jackson Health System (JHS) relied solely on the University of Miami Miller School of Medicine for all its research and nearly all its physicians. JHS suffered greatly from stagnation (from an IT perspective). However, in 2011 with new leadership, we turned that around, negotiated new agreements with UM, established agreements with FIU and began an internship program with the Miami-Dade College School of Nursing. Among the agreements established was a long-term agreement with Cerner, one of the major medical system software providers, for their entire comprehensive suite of software and systems.

The replacement of leadership also included the leadership in Information Technology. JHS IT has invested heavily in data farm technology, neural network server technology, and developed a team of data and computer scientists to begin designing and building artificial intelligence basis applications in the form of reusable algorithm modules. We have also developed an interface engine through which all data gathered flows and is routed so we can glean de-identified medical record data for use in the future. The artificial intelligence tool developed by our team led by George Rosello is called Overwatch.

Overwatch has been used to identify patients who use our very busy Emergency Department as primary care. We have been able to move many of these patients into insurance programs for improved Population Health. We have also used it to help match transplant patients to organs by taking over the manual process of checking and alerting.

For the last two years as the IT Project Manager for the JHS construction projects which includes the construction of two new hospitals and renovations of four others. I have been systematically constructing the infrastructure to connect every medical device in our facilities to our network. Cognizant of changes in processor performance and the emergence of innovative storage technologies, as well as improvements in high bandwidth – low latency networks, and fueled by the knowledge that all the medical equipment providers have begun selling equipment directly compatible with our Cerner electronic medical system enabling near-real-time assimilation of data, working in concert with the Chief Information Officer, Mike Garcia and the SVP of Construction Bill Seed, I have been systematically installing the most advanced infrastructure of any health care facility in the world. This collaborative effort fundamentally helps

> *Artificial intelligence seems not to originate from some outlandish formula, but rather from the patient, almost brute force of simple, straight forward algorithms.*
> *– Etham Alpaydin*

generate better healing outcomes because the research is applied as part of the original plan, as opposed to an afterthought once the project is complete.

Translational Medicine is defined as an interdisciplinary field of biomedical research supported by three pillars whose goal is to combine disciplines, resources, expertise, and technology. (Kyle Kurpinski, January 2014) The desired outcome is to promote enhancements in prevention, diagnosis, and therapies. (Sten Lindahl, 2018) Similarly, in health care information technology, introducing Translational Computer Science (David Abramson, 2019) will balance and augment traditional computer science research.

When complete next year, the new Christine E Lynn Rehabilitation Center at Jackson Health System will have complete 'smart room' technologies allowing physicians and researchers alike to have access to real-time data and analysis. Our Artificial Intelligence tools such as Overwatch, using this data will help improve outcomes for groups like the Miami Project to Cure Paralysis.

This strategy applies to all the medical, surgical, and mental health services we offer. In combination with medical record data, the data collected from myriad medical devices, bedside, handheld, wearable, and diagnostic (including radiological and magnetic imaging) will be systematically searched for the causes of diseases.

Another beneficial outcome of the project I am proposing in this book, will be the ability to recommend innovative cures. This project uses both artificial intelligence technologies as well as collective human intelligence.

The project to connect all medical devices to the EMR nets data provided in real-time on patients. Adding artificial intelligence using ML deep learning processes when the patient is admitted, and monitoring begins, enables rapid alerting relative to the medical state of the patient resulting in better healing outcomes.

This is one of many health systems.

It is not surprising to find out that the number of disciplines required to create an artificial intelligence such as this project proposes, is huge. Just the machine learning portion of this artificial intelligence project presents astronomical complexity because the understanding of the world through the data inputs that our computers will be receiving is massive and multifaceted. Think of the number of decision points you constantly make without thinking about them for instance while you are doing something simple like walking!

This project recognizes that no single health system, no matter how strong, has the ability to provide all the resources and all the disciplines and all the information and all the data that is required to provide health care information technology total value delivery. Therefore, this project proposes to tie many teams together using open source and the internet.

One of the most profound lessons I take away daily from being involved in the construction projects at Jackson Health System is the sheer complexity of the healing building. The myriad trades, disciplines, professionals, designers, constructors, materials, methods, and apparatus that are required to build one of these buildings is mind boggling. Similarly, this project must pull together the myriad sources and resources none being more important than the other.

Finally, the shear effort of normalizing this data will require machine learning algorithms. Luckily, over the last two decades the technology of machine learning to process that data into usable knowledge has advanced greatly. (Alpaydin, 2016)

In this project, we will put this into action.

Chapter 4 – The Search

Search Constructs

This project proposes to build artificial intelligence constructs for the purpose of searching the data developed in chapter three. The purpose of the search is to find the cause of and a means to eradicate infant leukemia. Jesus told us to seek and we would find. I know many who read this will not be religious, but I think he was one of the greatest teachers of all time.

We are hoping by the end of chapter three, that all the data we have collected is well defined and normalized. However, we know this is unlikely and are very likely to struggle with this going forward. Hopefully, data scientists who have reviewed chapter three are already working on this problem.

Seek and you will find. – Matthew 7:7

In this chapter we cannot suppose that the problem is well defined. To do so would pre-suppose that all who have gone before us are incompetent or less capable than we. We do not suppose this, on the contrary we look at this work as building on theirs. We are standing on the shoulders of giants and reaching for the heavens.

Given a specific problem, if we have the means for checking a projected solution, it follows we should be able to solve the problem by testing all possible answers. (Minsky, 1960) In this case though, we do not know if we are facing a specific problem or a group of problems and we may not even know what the correct question is. As I pointed out in chapter three in the Greaves and Kinlen studies, they could have been looking at the same cause through the prism of separate disciplines, which was the argument in chapter three, or they could have been viewing two problems with the same outcome.

This process would require too many hours of programming by individuals that possess skills sets that are too rare. We will only succeed by employing machine learning (ML) constructs. Of course, this may also imply that each problem is presented in an organized way, making it easier to decide if a proposed solution is acceptable. This is not out of the scope of possibility but is perhaps out of the scope of our current reality. It is possible that doctors and/or researchers participating in this project will have the knowledge and experience to frame such a well-defined problem. However, I think it is more likely we will be using artificial intelligence methods including machine learning to help develop these well-defined problems.

Cleveland Clinic has doctors who are coders by night. One such effort led to an AI search that led to a new way of treating cancer patients.
– Edward Marx, Chris Donovan

To search through all possibilities is not an efficient use of resources, human or machine. We will need to produce a sample data set. We often use the number of moves in a chess game as an example of the complexity, but this may be closer to the potential moves in the game "Go". In chess after both players move, there are four hundred possible board setups that exist. After the second pair of turns, there are one hundred ninety-seven thousand seven hundred forty-two possible games, and after three moves, one hundred twenty-one million. In Go however, on average, there are a hundred moves in every position; the imaginable number of possible games corresponds to around a number equal to the count of every atom in the known universe.

Similarly, when we are searching for the cause(s) of infant leukemia there are likely to be as many variables as there are in the game of Go.

This project is principally interested in problem solving methods which can be extended to more difficult problems. It is accepted that most systems which involve combinational processes usually grow exponentially more difficult as an artificial intelligence thereby sucking up additional computing resources as we add variables to the algorithms. Hill-climbing systems or local search systems, (Russell, 2003) studied under the names of adaptive or self-optimizing servo mechanisms may also be part of this search algorithm. Therefore, ruling out undue complexity, this project proposes to keep it simple.

The question then is, how much different is the searching we're doing than the searching Turing was doing when he broke the Enigma code in the Second World war? Certainly, the variables of the Enigma code were substantial, but I believe that this is significantly more complex than the Enigma code was. As Etham Alpaydin points out artificial intelligence seems not to originate from more unconventional and elaborate formulas but rather the patient, almost brute force of simple straight-forward algorithms (Alpaydin, 2016) applied over and over again against the search data or criteria. To me this seems very similar to what Turing was doing with his mechanical computer in the 1940s.

The plan is to first search and categorize the huge data into categories of big data, working to "chunk it down" (Lindley, 1966) into workable datasets categorized by behaviors, genetics, locations, age groups, ethnicity, socioeconomic situation, etc. This is also known as 'shallow parsing.' If this is artificial intelligence, then we can reason that it will work similar to human intelligence. Humans often need to chunk problems down into more manageable pieces. We are not proposing to use computers to replace human intelligence but to use these tools to assist us in accomplishing tasks that are difficult or impossible for us to do alone. This project proposes collective intelligence that includes many disciplines augmented by artificial intelligence constructs.

We could begin by using statistical mathematics as our primary method for search, in order to determine a subset of the full population of data, and thereby establish the Gaussian curve representing the frequency of data within the normal set. However, it is logical that there would be multiple 'local peaks' which are not true or satisfactory to the optimum of what a sample would statistically be. Therefore, we would be forced to try larger steps or changes. (Minsky, 1960) This makes me question if there is any reason to think a statistical search is viable. I am not making an argument either way, only that this project should review it and it should not be ruled out until the project has made a scientific determination as to its validity.

> *"Insanity is doing the same thing over and over and expecting different results."*
> *Albert Einstein*

It is often supposed that this false peak problem is the chief obstacle in machine learning, though this method can certainly be wearisome, for significant problems, such as this, it seems the more fundamental problem lies in finding a significant peak at all. Unfortunately, the "mesa phenomenon" or plateauing comes into play, Minsky described this as a time-space where small changes in a parameter usually leads to either no change in the outcome or to a large change in the outcome. The time-space is thus composed primarily of flat regions or "mesas" where no practical forward motion is obtained. We will need to be vigilant in this project as we attempt to avoid getting caught in the mesa phenomenon, even if it means abandoning that line of research until we have a better assessment of the data, better data, or even abandoning it all together.

One of the largest biases of humans is the tendency to hold on to a project (or part of a project) in an endless effort to succeed when the potential for success has already diminished past zero. We tend to become emotionally biased toward the belief that if we try one more time it will somehow work.

An example of this is the Sunk Cost Fallacy. (Sweis, 2018) The amount of time already spent on a task influences human choice about whether to continue. This persistent effort, money, resources and time are known as the "sunk cost." The more of these that exist, the more likelihood of resistance to giving up the pursuit of success, even when there is no indication of likely reward. We will endeavor not to get stuck on a mesa.

Marvin Minsky suggests building a "trial generator" to make small steps on results to reduce aimless wandering without compensating informational gains. This is a sort of machine learning tool that would "watch" the machine learning performance and make recommendations based on projected outcomes by sampling conditions at various points in the neural network.

This proposal is not intended to get into the deep technological planning for potential outcomes. I do not want to be so specific as to limit the methodologies, thoughts, or actions of the potential participants by framing the process of building constructs too rigidly.

Searching means examining every possible outcome until a true and provable answer is found, that could be a cause to avoid, a genetic anomaly, a trigger disease, a mineral in the soil, a molecule in a dust particle, or even the development of a vaccine.

Search and we will find.

Chapter 5 - Pattern Recognition

Pattern recognition

We will get more deeply invested in pattern recognition in this chapter as we deal with the concept of recognizing patterns, characters and images in pictures, as well as language, characters, context, and intent. However, in this chapter, pattern recognition also applies to finding similarities in the data that help us classify and categorize the data, to chunk it down.

For our purposes I am breaking Pattern Recognition into two broad categories.

- First is the computer technology of pattern recognition, this includes recognizing handwriting, typing, voice recordings, dictation, music, and all other linguistic methods of communication. This will include computer vision which, by extension includes image recognition such as pictures, video, and most important to this project, assimilation of digital x-Ray, CT, and MRI images.
- Second is something I am calling human life pattern recognition which includes social media and user volunteered data, for purposes of this project this is data associated with life events shared with us.

Natural language processing

The process of deploying NLP in the health care environment will progress in three steps designed to lower the barriers of entry, promote acceptance and adoption, and fully integrate with our project. By building the technological infrastructure of the network, servers and storage and normalizing data, we continue a strategy that is focused on artificial intelligence. We are building algorithms and tools that are being deployed in places where they are helping our providers improve outcomes. Jackson Health System is not alone, health systems across the country and across the world are similarly employed.

Continuing this long tradition leaders in health care will decrease the time it takes from our physicians' schedules for research by augmenting the process of reading and learning from peer reviewed papers using Natural Language Processing to help them glean the knowledge more quickly and effectively, producing a better quality environment for them and better outcomes for our patients. This process will be further beneficial as we comb through the medical records for causes and cures for diseases, in particular infant leukemia, while searching for recommended methods and practices that help reduce costs and increase revenues. While we are delivering narrative summaries to the doctors, we are also assimilating the data for search.

Current NLP technology borrows from several, varied fields, requiring today's NLP researchers and developers to broaden their mental knowledgebase significantly. This means our project must attract talent beyond the scope of most health systems.

As an example: artificial intelligence is good at the repetitive routine processes. The first application that really got a lot of attention was document classification in the discovery phase of a trial. Pretrial litigation often includes a request from the opposition to produce all the documents that are responsive to a particular subject. Attorneys then have to go through the entire volume of documents and determine which ones are responsive and which ones are not. As people went to digital documents, the volumes of documents that had to be searched, became huge. Therefore, it became very expensive. This caused a lot of pressure to automate the process. Initially the automation took the form of looking for keywords, but key words are problematic because, similar to health care, a given idea or a given concept can be expressed in a lot of different ways. If you don't have the right key word, you're going to miss it.

Eventually what happened was a machine learning application, where the set of lawyers will take a sample of the documents that have been classified and they will classify that sample. Then you're running a machine learning natural language processing algorithm on that sample to identify what pattern of words or combinations of words or words in three strings together and are forming the protocol for these legal documents. This application of the process can be extended to multiple strings in order to refine the algorithmic process. Though this saved time, determining what is responsive, and what is not, this is responsive with probably 80% or is this is responsive with a probability of 90%. If it is a probability of 90% the resulting human decision is to just turn it over to the other side and that's the end of it. If the estimation probability of it being responsive is 40% or less the documents are retained. The documents between 41% and 89% are going to have human review to determine whether or not these documents to get turned over. (Levy, 2019)

Similar to the example above, this project will use natural language processing to read the massive volume of documents that are transcribed as medical records over the past several decades. Our process will be similar, as we will evaluate those documents against sample documents to generate a score to assist us in eliminating all the documents that have no relevant data for this project. We will, however, store all those documents in a database for later use. Similarly, we may find a reason to classify those documents for later use.

One of the large issues we will encounter with handwritten medical records, is handwritten rules handle 'ungrammatical' spoken prose and (in medical contexts) the highly telegraphic prose of in-hospital progress notes are often poorly composed due to workload, fatigue, and verbal 'shorthand', although such prose is easily human-comprehensible. (Prakash M. Nadkarni, 2011) Unlike the legal profession example used, we face substantially

---

Early simplistic approaches, for example, word for word Russian to English machine translation, were defeated by homographs and identically spelled words with multiple meanings and metaphors, leading to the Bible quote, 'the spirit is willing, but the flesh is weak' being translated to 'the vodka is agreeable, but the meat is spoiled.'

---

different challenges, like sentence boundary detection, tokenization, part of speech assignment to individual words, and morphological decomposition.

Additionally, we will overcome spelling and grammatical errors, homophones, phrases, word phrase order issues, and derivations. There are, however, resources to help us with this, including the National Institutes of Health, the National Library of Medicine and the Unified Medical Language System. I encourage those interested to review the following article: Journal of American Medical Informatics Association by Dr. Prakash M. Nadkami, Yale University School of Medicine.

Computer vision

Computer visual recognition tasks have different intricacies. In this chapter we're not dealing with reading bar codes which is one of the simplest methods for computers to read because very little data is actually stored in bar code format. Bar codes play a huge role in health care to assure patients are properly treated, for example, two factor authentication assures the correct medication. Those verifications read into the patient record enabling us to be very sure the treatment protocol is accurate.

Computer vision, simply stated, is what the computer 'sees' through cameras or other sensors. Whether bar code or other character recognitions the computer reads by means of sensors. The when scanning documents, the computer sees a matrix of spatial locations that are translated into ones or zeros. These spatial locations can be translated into binary vectors allowing computers to see colors and shades. Current methods have a number of different issues within this description. First, computers more frequently see in a scope that does not exist in the human eye, where we would see a single thought, computers view every space allowed as matrix of spatial locations. Depending on how that matrix is vectorized it will have shades defined that range from black to white, each of those is represented by a vector of zeros and ones that tell the computer that this space is something to 'read'. The computer is looking for edges, that represent bends and strokes of various orientations that has regularity that it can capture as a character. We can then programmatically compare this to a training set of characters and determine what that character is. For instance, if reading a 'dirty paper' discoloration, folds, bug dots, and any number of other anomalies can cause the computer's vision to misread the character. It has to do with finding the edge, determining what is the curve, determining what is a character. This is why the Optical Character Recognition (OCR) set of characters was developed. It is easier to have a scenario, where a known character set is used. This also why simple fonts like courier work better than New Time Roman. What computers see versus what we see will be important in this project. (Alpaydin, 2016)

Similarly, a computer doesn't see colors or depth or contrast it sees pixels individual bits on a screen or in a pattern so it's part of the pattern recognition, the end all being converting text of all types and images of all types, into meaningful, searchable data. This project anticipates scanning in documents and hoping to have natural language processing (NLP) and pattern recognition help us turn paper documents into digital documents that are usable as a database for us to search.

That applies also the handwritten documents, for instance, let's think of the difference between cursive versus printed text. As an example; if I handwrite a document printing it out with individual box characters, using all capital letters; first can I train against other similar documents, however,

The data that social media users generate by creating and interacting with web-based information ... provide a new data source for research. - Katja Reuter

how different are my various documents? What happens if I switch it up in the document and use cursive for a few characters or words? What if I can't spell particularly well? I am writing a medical report, what if I abbreviate or use shorthand? Additionally, what if the dictation of the doctor to the medical record there's something simple like "the patient suffers from a broken finger" versus "there is a small fracture in the left index phalange of the patient?" While these two sentences say essentially the same thing, they are not the same as far as classification for a computer system is concerned.

So how do I use a training set of documents with my own handwriting as an example to take all the documents that I have handwritten and enable the computer to scan those and turn them into usable digital information? I have used this as a simple example so we can begin to understand the issues of converting these handwritten medical records to digital media. This will be compounded by many doctors writing these medical records. Typed will be easier, but this is a very large challenge.

This is one of our computer vision challenges. The other challenge is the digital images such as x-ray and MRI. The manufacturers of these devices are experiencing some level of success on this. Manufactures such as GE, Philips and Siemens are developing and producing artificial intelligence constructs that assist the radiologists in recognizing the subtleties of the medical scans to help reach accurate diagnoses. (Sejnowski, 2018)

Human life

Then there is the more interesting level of pattern recognition. What happened in the patient's life that led to this diagnosis? Are there similarities in lifestyles, locations, food, parks visited, facilities attended, etc. that have also been similarly affected in the lives of other patients?

As an example: A child is born in Dallas Texas. The child is diagnosed with infant leukemia at 10 months of age. This child was conceived and born in an area near the airport. During that time there was a malfunction in a nearby power plant that lasted for fifteen hours before it was repaired. There are three other children within five miles of the plant that were diagnosed within a month of each other. Also, during that time there was a chemical spill into a nearby creek that fed the Trinity River. A telephone company main trunk cable was broken for several hours bleeding small amounts electromagnetic radiation into the air. Finally, a road service company repaved the main road through the neighborhood, one of the mineral components of the paving material used was contaminated with a carcinogen. Three of the four patients ate a specific restaurant. These too are patterns to be recognized.

Furthermore, Twitter, Facebook, Instagram and other social media sites offer platforms for people to transmit information, thoughts, and emotional state about their daily lives. Since Twitter messages (called tweets) often reflect in-the-moment updates, they're filled with useful comments and material about the relational world. Researchers have examined a range of social applications based on tweets, ranging from political posts to earthquake monitoring, that have demonstrated Twitter's ability to deliver fast, cheap, and reliable tools for monitoring real-time events. (Dredze, 2012) This project will include such voluntary evidence.

It is worthwhile to include that this is not the only project that uses such data. The use of social media to support public health is a substantial potential tool in the data base of current knowledge. Despite the potential success in investigative studies, there are limited studies on inferences and little use of social media in practice. However, information gleaned from the social media posts demonstrates the effectiveness of social media in supporting and improving public health and in identifying target information. A primary recommendation resulting from the review is to identify opportunities that enable public health professionals to integrate social media analytics into disease surveillance and outbreak management practice. (Katja Reuter, 2018)

So, overlaying all the methodologies, we find a way to use pattern recognition to not only read the data entered on paper and electronic medical records but also to search for patterns of behavior, local environmental conditions, genetics, and relationships.

Whether using this technology to analyze the facial expressions of a patient in a telemedicine environment using a facial recognition algorithm, pattern recognition to determine characters, or vectorizing the data into datasets to run through machine learning constructs, we have a substantial effort ahead of us in this project. Information seeking is a cognitive, psychological and physical activity. (Chirag Shah, 2014)

Chapter 6 - Learning

Computer learning has long been the goal computer scientists. The quest to build an "artificial brain" (AI) is one of the outstanding challenges of modern computer science. Humanity's habitual attempts to imitate the human brain have often, if not continuously, been reflected in the leading technology of the era. Until recently the technology did not actually begin to exist.

Over the last decade IBM has gone from near zero to sixty-four million neurons being available in artificial neural networks in IBM's True North project. (Michael V.DeBole, 2019)

Some of this springs from the efforts to bridge the disparity between computers and the brain in the field of neuromorphic engineering when Carver Mead observed the biological neurons and silicon transistors share similar device physics. (S.C. Liu, 2010) In 2008 Doctor Todd Hylton at the Defense Advanced Research Projects Agency (DARPA) launched a program for electronic neuromorphic machine technology that is scalable to biological levels. (Hylton, 2011) A decade later the ambitious vision of DARPA was realized by IBM in the True North brain inspired processor. Today True North is in the hands of hundreds of researchers and more than fifty institutions in five continents. As a result, True North has been inducted into the computer History Museum. The above is given to show the recent advancements in computing technologies that are available to this project. I cite this only as an example of the improvements in technology that are enabling the resurgence of artificial intelligence. The main component of which, in my opinion, is machine learning (ML) that in turn is enabled by the ability to build neural networks.

Deep neural networks have realized inspiring achievements of intelligence, greater than humans in specific tasks and attaining high effectiveness at speech recognition, machine translation, as examples think of Siri's and Alexa's capabilities. Similarly, higher level machine human-like cognitive activities such as interpretation and classification of such visual objects as photos we store on Google's photo application demonstrate the strength of machine learning. Although there are many successful architectural models using Deep Neural Networks (DNNs) their common distinguishing model uses many layers of hidden nodes to build deep topology constructs of nonlinear neurons, with linearly weighted connections, trained by back propagation to differentiate complex inputs to a higher degree of precision. (Steven D. Pyle, 2019)

However, this characteristic, (having many layers) demands high computational capability and very large memory configurations. This tends to be costly, in this project we will be investigating the possibility of attaining similar recognition capabilities in large format internet based collaborative neural network constructs. We may be using reduced precision approaches at first, but as we discussed earlier it may be more effective to use many simple iterations of effective algorithms, Alpaydin's "brute force" artificial intelligence. This would potentially mean a construct that has significantly lower computation memory demands from a single computer or network. By reducing these base requirements in situational networks there is a potential the needed total resources could be realized in resource constrained platforms such as mobile and Internet of Things devices.

Stochasticity applies to these deep learning machine learning processes. We are counting on uncovering unimagined, randomly determined outcomes that will lead us to the answers or help us determine the questions to ask.

In order not to try all possibilities we must be resourceful, using machine learning to classify problem situations into categories associated with fields of effectiveness of the different procedures. (Minsky, 1960) These pattern recognition methods must extract heuristically significant features of the objects they are learning from. The simplest methods match the object against standards or prototypes and are related to supervised learning methodologies. Employing supervised methods, we can subject each object of the sequence to machine learning tests, each detecting some property in heuristic importance. Two important difficulties arise here: inventing new useful properties and combining many properties to form a recognition system. Hence, the need for supervised learning. (Sejnowski, 2018)

Machine learning is the most important recent capability. Success in this project the machine learning constructs we build will be the key to that success.

Bias

Human bias translates into machine learning. Bias is not necessarily intentional. Where focus goes the process flows (Newport, 2016)In writing this book I encountered such a scenario. I overlooked a friend, because he had not been integral to my recent projects. Yet he alone would have been and will be in the future, a major contributor to this work. We will have to be cognizant of bias and work to overcome it in this project.

Chapter 7 - Planning

In Chapter 1, we examined the reason for this great work, this project to do something far beyond our individual power. Only by working together collaboratively with the machines we have created will we succeed.

In Chapter 2, I explained the core concept of using this project to build constructs. The purpose of the constructs is to make them interchangeable and reusable.

In Chapter 3, we looked over the sources of data and discussed the process of normalizing that data so that it would be usable in the project.

In Chapter 4, we scrutinized the search process and added to it the scope of leveraging the professionals in the business such as the resident doctors who might be interested in being doctors during the day and coders at night.

In Chapter 5, I went through some of the problems and methods we might be confronted with in the process of using pattern recognition to decode the manually generated data as well as the web-based data sources.

In Chapter 6, we touched on machine learning. This chapter only touches on the subject, hopefully enough to trigger the thought processes necessary to stir the interest of the data scientists needed by this project as well as the executives needed to back it.

In this chapter we are not going to talk about computer planning in any depth. Although I think we will need to use these technologies to assist us in the planning.

Introducing artificial intelligence technologies to the environment at Jackson Health System and other health systems in America offers many benefits and very few detriments. The benefit to researchers working directly with artificial intelligence technologies will likely be as impressive and groundbreaking as the benefits to radiologists discussed by Professor Rus of MIT. More than any single tool ever provided to the medical profession's doctors, nurses, and technicians, and indeed to patients, is the artificial intelligence construct tool kit. From employing NLP to search medical records and historical documents to real time ML and deep learning algorithms working through the multitude of feeds from medical devices, humanity will benefit from the collaboration with this powerful machine-based tool set.

There will be a learning curve particularly in areas relating to supply chain management and revenue cycle where we will implement artificial intelligence tools to monitor and record the movement and utilization of inventory items. The flow of implanted items for surgical procedures will be dramatically improved. While this will not eliminate jobs, it will require certain upskill training. However, upskilling is something we do all the time in health care.

New IT jobs will be created to support this. Bringing nurses and doctors into IT will need to continue.

Human machine integration
How will the work be divided?

Jackson Health System represents a workforce of twelve thousand or more people concentrating on the health care. Not all are clinicians, but all have a singular mission to provide the best level of health care available anywhere. Imagine introducing to that culture the understanding of what artificial intelligence really is and really offers. Image bright young doctors who work as physicians during the day and coders at night! Imagine the contributions of enlightened nurses. Imagine a medical workforce who is

49

already looking for answers given the artificial intelligence

---

*You do not understand something until you can
explain it to your grandmother.
- Albert Einstein*

---

tool set. Imagine if it could be demystified and explained in
terms they could quickly grasp and begin to assimilate into
their daily profession.

What roles will people play and where do the computational
devices fit? People are miracles looking for a place happen!
People are deeply motivated to heal wherever they can heal
and identify better methods to ease the disease. We are
learning, we aren't there yet, but we can teach them to
understand and help them to use and even develop the tools.

Albert Einstein once said, "You don't understand something
unless you can explain it to your grandmother." It is time to
explain it.

The time is now.

Considerations of Machine Learning

In health care we see people at their worst and at their best.
It is reasonable to assume that an artificial intelligence
without the moral leadership of a human counterpart could
form a bias that is not healing.

As an example, an artificial intelligence might form a bias
that all smokers should simply be put to death, they are
going to die anyway from cancer so the cure for that cancer
is eliminate the diseased population and spend no more
money on them.

Similarly, an improperly constructed set of algorithms may not recognize the value of the signal inputs from the monitoring equipment on the bedside and could (theoretically) be used to increase (or decrease) saline solution or turn off the patient's ability to self-medicate.

If an ML application were improperly weighted, could it make recommendations for treatments based on the biases of nurse or other clinician who had extreme religious convictions, even though his or her human counterparts did not pick up on the subtle clues, the NLP did?

These are all extreme. There is an old middle eastern saying, "They strain at a gnat and swallow a camel." In health care, we are governed by the Hippocratic Oath to do no harm, artificial intelligence will make recommendations and humans will use that tool to help diagnose diseases and cure patients, but it will be a human decision not that of a computer.

A more likely case is a tired nurse, medicating an allergic patient based on an erroneous order from a tired physician. The nurse scans the barcode on the medication, an artificial intelligence notices the problem, turns the monitor screen red alarming the nurse and physician, saving the patient suffering, even death.

Chapter 8 – Induction
Setting the Vision

To help maintain the vision and help avoid plateauing in this project we will maintain our focus on viable outcomes without bias. In his 1985 book "Competitive Advantage: Creating and Sustaining Superior Performance" Michael Porter set out three generic strategies. Applying these strategies to the implementation of the artificial intelligence constructs described in this chapter demonstrates the validity of the business case as it applies to Health Care Information Technology Total Value Delivery.

Health care has always been a leader in pioneering new and novel approaches to healing. Our unique focus on our mission to provide a single, high quality standard of care for our communities is augmented and enhanced by discovering new and better methods to identify and eliminate catastrophic diseases such as infant leukemia. By applying artificial intelligence constructs, we minimize the cost of research to the organizations as well as help to minimize the cost of treatment to the patients and their families. At the same time, while not wanting to bog the scientific part of this project down with financial concerns, money will play a role in the success of this project.

We must remain focused on the most important process we can improve in health care information technology and that is finding the cause of and innovative cures for infant leukemia. I think the artificial intelligence constructs we build in this project will be used for similar searches and will discover similar outcomes for any number of other devastating diseases. Through the application of re-usable artificial intelligence technology search constructs, we will be discovering causes of and seeking innovative cures for infant and childhood leukemia as well as other devastating childhood and adult diseases. The outcome for developing this technology is beneficial to all of humanity.

Applying artificial intelligence constructs developed in this project to the bedside medical device integrations we will enhance differentiation with peers as we improve healing outcomes, reduce hospital stay durations, and increase patient satisfaction; while reducing the cost of the patient's stay, enabling this to be a self-funding project overall. (Kyle Kurpinski, January 2014)

Additionally, we will continue to reduce the cost of surgical procedures by constantly improving the process of supplying the surgically necessary products, allowing surgeons to spend less time defining their surgical preferences per procedure type while reducing wasted devices and manual inventory efforts. I believe these will all be by-products of developing the artificial intelligence constructs we build for this project.

Developing Technical Leadership

In my 2017 book "Health Care Information Technology Integrated Project Delivery" I outlined a method for beginning projects with deep collaboration with the stakeholders. We will apply this methodology in the artificial intelligence projects here. (Tuohy, 2017)

The success of this project depends on the collective intelligence of both the Information Technology computer scientists, systems integration specialists, data scientists, and programmers as well physicians, nurses, medical technicians, medical researchers, and scientists, as well as revenue cycle and executive leadership all aided by artificial intelligence.

Continued executive sponsorship and an active executive leadership role are required in this project. Executive participation provides vision and inspiration for the entire team. The project team will be assisted by a project integration coach in a lean and agile approach to project management.

This project represents another step in the evolutionary advancement of health care information technology that health care is already pursuing. It sustains the business model of most health system CEOs, of being the best, most efficient and most effective health care system in their respective regions and supports the Population Health Initiative.

We have already invested heavily in the infrastructure, servers, and storage necessary to support this project, however, continued commitment to the maintenance and growth of the technical infrastructure as well as the human intelligence involved is required. Currently, available architectures for the neural networking are robust and scalable, deep collaboration among teams using the internet will help spread the costs of operating this project across a broad spectrum of organizations.

We will continue to nurture and sustain our partnerships with the universities and with our EMR and clinical systems providers. We will also continue to develop and maintain vendors and manufacturers of medical devices that are certified compatible by our EMR provider, and those devices will all be network connected.

Now is the time to assign names to the roles in this project, to garner time commitments from the individuals (and their managers) who will participate, and to begin planning and developing teams.

This roadmap is not only a project plan. What is total value delivery in health care? Total value delivery is the process of healing, not only providing help in catastrophic events such as traumatic injury or surgical necessity but also in the identification of causes of disease (such as infant leukemia) so these diseases may be eliminated. Health care Information Technology (HIT) employing machine learning technologies, stands in a unique position enabled by recent breakthroughs in hardware and algorithms to assist in these goals.

This project represents the next step in the evolutionary advancement of health care information technology that Jackson Health System and other health systems are already pursuing. It also sustains the business model of our CEOs of being the best, most efficient and most effective health care system in their respective regions and being the desired destination for treatment. Further, it augments and supports the Population Health Initiative.

We have already invested heavily in the infrastructure, servers, and storage necessary to support similar projects, however, continued commitment to the maintenance and growth of the technical infrastructure as well as the human intelligence involved is required. Our architecture for neural networking is robust and scalable and in conjunction with our collective human intelligence, will provide an unequalled atmosphere of learning. This learning is fueled by an incredible amount of existing data as well as an ever-increasing level of data accumulation from every bedside device and monitor in the system. New technologies are incorporating wearable devices and locally maintained health history such as that collected on one's smart phone.

Doctors will no longer be limited to the data they are able to collect while a patient is in their office, they will have vitals for as long as the wearable device or smart phone have been recording it.

Using the principals of Integrated Project Delivery, we will foster deep collaboration and diversity knowing this is the basis of human collective intelligence. We will reinforce this and augment it with artificial intelligence tool sets and constructs. We will continue to nurture and sustain our partnerships with the universities and with our Electronic Medical Record (EMR) and clinical systems provider. We will also continue to develop and maintain vendors and manufacturers of medical devices that are certified compatible by our respective EMR provider, and those devices will all be network connected. Enabling ever increasing opportunities for human and computer intellectual advancement. Mimicking the processes at Cleveland Clinic, we will encourage the development of specialized knowledge coders such as doctors who practice medicine during the day and code in their off hours.

Direction for the future

One of the challenges of change is involving the people who do not understand its value. This is particularly true of Jackson Health System where workloads are sometimes overwhelming. Walking into an environment like this with a proposal to 'improve' things is often met with skepticism. Historically, IT has promised to make work easier and reduce paperwork. Executive participation and leadership is crucial to project success.

To succeed in this project, IT will need to collaborate more deeply and embrace those who would participate, even at the level of coding. In a recent MIT SMR webinar, Edward Marx and Chris Donovan discussed some of the things happing at Cleveland Clinic, like physicians who practice medicine during the day and code at night. This line of thinking stands in stark contrast to the conventional silos that have been in place for so long. As we work together to better understand each other's needs, we will produce better artificial intelligence products that will more completely fill those needs. All of us working collaboratively will learn more collectively and so become a better team.

Technical and regulatory challenges also exist that must be addressed and (sometimes) overcome. There are issues of data ownership, privacy and integrity. From the perspective of technology in health care, there are data sources that may or may not have a model of data output that can be considered normalized, but the data has value all the same. Interface engines will need to be able to assist in normalizing data from bedside devices, wearable devices, handheld and optical devices. Nonstandard software may play an integral part of specific regiments of care, this data must also be normalized to create a complete representation and at the heart of all this, NLP will be the artificial intelligence tool used to write the narrative.

Shall we begin?

References

Alpaydin, E. (2016). *Machine Learning*. Cambridge, MA: MIT Press.

Chirag Shah, R. C. (2014, March). Collaborative Information Seeking. *IEEE Computer*, 22-25.

David Abramson, M. P. (2019). Translational Research in Computer Science. *IEEE Computer*, 16-23.

Dredze, M. (2012). How Social Media Will Change Public Health. *Computer*, 1572-1672.

Greaves, M. (Aug 2018). A casual mechanism for childhood acute lymphoblastic leukemia. *Nature Reviews*, 471-484.

Hylton, T. (2011, April 8). *DARPA Works to Build Computers Inspired by Human Brain*. Retrieved from Armedwith Science: https://science.dodlive.mil/2011/04/08/darpa-works-to-build-computers-inspired-by-human-brain/

Katja Reuter, P. A.-K. (2018). Monitoring Twitter Conversations for Targeted Recruitment in Cancer Trials in Lod Angeles County: Protocol for Mixed-Methods Pilot Study. *JMIR Research Protocols*.

Kinlen, L. (Dec 1988). Evidence for an infective cause of childhood leukemia. *The Lancet*, 1323-1327.

Kline, R. (2011, April). Cybernetics, Automata Studies, and the Dartmouth Conference on Artificial Intelligence. *IEEE Annals of the History of Computing, 33*(4), 5-16. doi:10.1109/MAHC.2010.44

Kyle Kurpinski, T. J. (January 2014). Mastering Translational Medicine: Interdisciplinary Education for a New Generation. *Science*, Vol 6 Issue 218.

Levy, F. (2019, March). Artificial Intelligence: Implications For Business Strategy - Module 3.

Lindley, R. (1966, Aug). Recoding as a function of chunking and meaningfulness. *Psychonomic Science, Volume 6*(Issue 8), 393-394. Retrieved from Wikipedia.

Marusak, H. (2019, July 24). Understanding the Psychological Effects of Childhood Cancer. *Scientific American*.

McCarthy, J. (2006, 10 30). *The Dartmouth Workshop--as planned and as it happened*. Retrieved from Stanford: www.formal.stanford.edu/jmc/slides/dartmouth/dartmouth/node1.html

McCarthy, M. R. (1955). *A Proposal for the Dartmouth Summer Research Project on Artifical Inetlligence*. Hanover, New Hampshire: Dartmouth College.

McChrystal, S. (2015). *Team of Teams*. New York: Penguin.

Michael V.DeBole, E. (2019, May). True North: Accellerating from Zero to 64 Million Nuerons in 10 Years. *Computer*, 20-29.

Minsky, M. (1960). Steps Toward Artificial Intelligence. *Proceedings of The IRE*, 8-30.

Mnih, V. (2015). Human-level control through deep reinforcement learning. *Nature*, 529-533.

Newport, C. (2016). *Deep Work*. New York, NY: Grand Central Publishing.

NIH. (2018, Sep 4). *NCI Dictionary of Cancer Terms*. Retrieved from NIH / National Cancer Institute: https://www.cancer.gov/publications/dictionaries/cancer-terms/def/event-free-survival

Prakash M. Nadkarni, L. O.-M. (2011). Natural language processing: an introduction. *Journal of American Medical Informatics Association, 18*, 544-551. doi:doi:10.1136/amiajnl-2011-000464

Russell, S. J. (2003). *Artificial Intelligence: A Modern Approach*. Upper Saddle River, NJ: Prentice-Hall.

S.C. Liu, T. D. (2010). Neuromorphic Sensory Systems. *Current Opionion Neurobiology, 20*(3), 288-295.

Sejnowski, T. J. (2018). *The Deep Learning Revolution*. Cambridge, Massachusetts: Massachusetts Intitute of Technology Press.

Sten Lindahl, F. M. (2018). *Translational medicine*. Encyclopædia Britannica, inc.

Steven D. Pyle, J. D. (2019). Leveraging Stocasticity for In Situ Learning in Binarized Deep Neural Networks. *IEEE Computer, 52*(5), 30-39.

Sweis, B. M. (2018). Sensitivity to "sunk costs" in mice, rats, and humans. *Science, 361*(6398), 178-181. doi:10.1126/science.aar8644

Trotter, F. (2013). *Hacking Healthcare*. Sebastopol, CA: O'Reilly Media.

Tuohy, T. (2017). *Healthcare Information Technology Itegrated Project Delivery*. Miami.

Turing, A. M. (1950). Computing Machinery and Intelligence. *Mind 49*, 433-460.

www.ingramcontent.com/pod-product-compliance
Lightning Source LLC
Chambersburg PA
CBHW021020180526
45163CB00005B/2044